The Quick Guide to Divorce Mediation

Practical Advice for Satisfying Agreements

Jon Peters

DEDICATION

This book is dedicated to the hundreds of parents who have taught me about the challenges of co-parenting children after separation. I am enlivened by their courage in the face of complexity.

PREFACE

Hello. I've been mediating divorces, especially for parents who share children, for over fifteen years. In my mediation practice, I provide a facilitative approach that focuses on agreements, but with a strong emphasis on reaching wise, satisfying agreements that reduce post-divorce conflict and make it more likely that the parties will avoid emotionally and financially costly litigation.

I strive to help my clients prepare for and negotiate mediation in the best way. However, I know mediation is often very confusing and stressful. Clients have reported dealing with an aggressive mediator on top of getting their buttons pushed by the other party or an attorney. If the mediator cares about your state of mind at all, it may seem that they just want to wear you out so you'll finalize an agreement, regardless of its quality. So, I offer this explanation and advice to help you understand and negotiate the mediation process to get the most satisfying outcome.

In this book, you'll find answers to the most common questions people have when considering mediation. I'll explain how to not only prepare for the mediation process, but also handle stress so that you don't run interference for yourself. You'll also find resources that may be helpful for further preparation for your mediated issues. Mediation is a very useful process for thousands of people every year. Research has shown mediation to save many people thousands of dollars by avoiding expensive litigation and people tend to report greater satisfaction with mediated agreements compared to litigated orders. I wish the best for you!

CONTENTS

ACKNOWLEDGMENTS

My dear friend, Adam Davis, has been instrumentally and emotionally supportive during this, and other, endeavors. Thanks to him, again!

INTRODUCTION

Mediation is often helpful during the divorce process. But, it can be confusing and stressful to choose whether to engage in mediation and how to negotiate the process. This book will explain mediation and offer advice about working toward the most satisfying agreements.

Chapters Two and Three will explain mediation and answer common questions that parties have prior to and during the mediation process. This will help you make a careful choice about whether and how to engage in the mediation process.

Chapter Four will help you understand how to prepare for and negotiate the mediation process in an optimal way. Not all mediations are successful. Many don't result in satisfying agreements that parties can rely on in the future. However, many people craft wise and lasting agreements through mediation. This can be valuable if it reduces a reliance on litigation to resolve disagreements. Litigation is typically more expensive than mutually agreed decisions. Fighting in court is damaging to ongoing relationships, something to consider especially if you need to continue to collaborate with the other party—say because of shared children.

Chapter Five will explain why it is essential to keep perspective through the mediation process. People often focus on the goals of mediation and lose sight of the potential consequences of damaging conflict. I'll explain how to put good legal advice into a wider view that also considers the ongoing relationship you may need to have with the other party, long after your divorce. This is especially true if you share children.

In Chapter Six, I'll talk about the issue of compromise in negotiation. Parties in mediation often get fixated on getting the other person to compromise. They may see compromise as the best type of mutual solution to a disagreement. But, I'll explain why meeting in the middle of two different positions is not always the best choice.

Chapter Seven focuses on handling stress during the mediation process. As will be explained, stress has a strong effect on the outcome of mediation. Of course, stress is unpleasant. Stress management during the mediation process might reduce some discomfort. But, importantly, dealing effectively with stress can support parties in crafting the best possible agreements. Understanding and working constructively with stress will help you participate in the best possible way. I hope this book helps you choose wisely what to bring to the table, craft mutually satisfying agreements, navigate the process with the least stress, and avoid expensive and damaging litigation.

WHAT IS MEDIATION?

If you are thinking about mediation, that means you are faced with making decisions around very consequential issues. These choices and agreements will impact you, and others, financially and emotionally. They might—if you are divorcing parents—impact the quality of life for you and your children for many years. Of course, you first want to decide whether mediation might be helpful for you. This chapter will answer many questions that people have about mediation. First, let's define mediation as *a specific type of conflict resolution process.*

Mediation is a process in which parties meet together with a neutral mediator toward the goal of crafting satisfying agreements. The role of the mediator differs from other professionals who might be involved in a case. The process and goals differ as well. Let's examine each part.

Mediators are neutral, not arbitrators of disagreements

Mediators are expected to be neutral in order to best support parties during the mediation process. Being neutral means *not taking a position in regards to positions brought by the parties.* As an example, two parents might be mediating the parenting time schedule of their shared child. In the process, the parents seem to move toward an agreement of 50/50 shared time. Perhaps the mediator has a positive or negative view of this type of schedule. The mediator's personal view of the 50/50 position should not interfere with the parties' ability to work toward a mutually acceptable agreement.

This is not to say that the mediator would support any possible position. In fact, to be ethical, the mediator should not continue to support a process that seems to lead to an unacceptable agreement. It is the mediator's responsibility to support a wide range of possible agreements, but not in an unlimited sense. A mediator will recuse her/himself in a situation where parties attempt to agree to something that is inherently unreasonable.

Another way to think about mediator neutrality is that he/she will avoid sharing expert advice, even if an expert. Most mediators are either attorneys or social workers/therapists. And, the mediator may have expertise in an area that has direct bearing on the mediated issues. This is often handled in the following ways.

Your mediator might ask you if you want them to offer *substantive input* during the process. If you indicate that you don't want any, they will likely remain fairly silent in terms of offering explicit ideas related to your issues. Or, they might voice ideas that you can consider. This is sometimes helpful if the mediator has experience with your particular issues. Here's an example of what that might look like:

When I have cases in which people are mediating parenting time schedules for their children, I will often offer ideas about a variety of ways that other parents have crafted schedules. Each parent often enters mediation with their own idea and try to convince the other parent to accept their position. But, often, considering other options ends up being more satisfying. The agreement is neither Plan A nor Plan B, but maybe Plan C...or Plan D, or E, or F! Having worked with hundreds of parents over the years, I have experience with many different scheduling arrangements. Parents who seek my input, get to hear about those options. Of course, it is you and the other party who will live with the mediated agreement, *not the mediator!* You should only finalize the agreement if you believe it will be workable for you and all involved.

So, mediation is not legal advice. It is also not mental health evaluation or treatment, even if your mediator is a social worker or therapist. It is also not *arbitration*, which is a process of conflict resolution where parties offer support for their positions and the arbitrator can render a binding decision. In mediation, if parties do not reach an agreement around a particular issue or set of issues, the mediator will not offer a resolution.

The mediation process is private

Parties in mediation sometimes have concerns about information from the process being shared with other parties or the courts. This concern is safeguarded by the codes and practices of mediation. This is typically explicitly constrained by state legal code. Mediators do not share notes about the process with any other party or the court. Mediators do not communicate directly with courts about the process. Agreements are the property of the parties who usually have the responsibility of communicating them with the court, if appropriate.

Typically, notes from mediators can't be obtained to use in court and mediators do not go to court to testify as witnesses. This constraint helps to protect parties in the mediation process. People involved in contentious litigation often seek input or testimony from collateral sources in order to support their legal positions. However, if mediators were to regularly attend court hearings to testify in ways that were unfavorable to parties involved, it would hinder the mediation process. Parties need to participate in good faith, but also without concern that the mediator will communicate something damaging later in the litigation process.

In some states, the mediator enjoys immunity from testimony in the same way as judges. If you have specific questions about this issue, read the code that applies to mediation or alternative conflict resolution in your state or consult your attorney. If you are worried that either attorney working in your case might try to subpoena the mediator or records from the process, discuss this concern with the mediator to see if they have dealt with that before or if they have a policy concerning quashing such a subpoena.

Can my mediator also be my attorney?

It is also the case that mediators will only play one role in a particular case. For example, if your mediator is an attorney, he or she will not represent you as an attorney even if the mediation process stops. This isolation of the mediator to one role is another method for safeguarding the mediation process.

We really don't want to fight, do we need a mediator?

Mediation is less adversarial than litigation. It often saves money compared to litigation. And, it tends to be less emotionally damaging to an ongoing relationship and lead to more lastingly satisfying agreements. And, it may not be necessary. In cases where parties are in dispute of one or more substantive issues, it is often quite helpful. It may save money and be less adversarial than a co-mediated issue, one where two attorneys communicate back and forth to reach an agreement. And, there is another choice that you should consider.

Recently, many people have been choosing Collaborative Divorce processes to avoid costly and damaging litigation. You may have collaborative divorce practices in your local area. I suggest visiting www.collaborativedivorce.net for more information. You can use online searches to find attorneys providing this service in your region. In the collaborative process, parties work together to avoid adversarial litigation processes and often save money by doing so. If you share children and want to avoid damaging your co-parenting relationship in the future, I suggest you consider this method.

Summary

Mediators are neutral. They will not arbitrate your disagreement, even if the mediation process fails. They will not function as attorneys or mental health professionals. Mediation is not legal advice or mental health evaluation. The process is private and the mediator will not testify in court or communicate about the process. The mediator will play only one role in your case. The agreement will need to be evaluated and submitted to the court, and this is the responsibility of the parties unless otherwise agreed with the mediator.

To find more in more discussion of many of the issues explained in this book, I suggest visiting www.mediate.com/about. There you can find many online articles with in depth explanations about a very wide range of mediation issues and also connections to local mediators.

THE PROCESS OF MEDIATION

How do we select a mediator?

Mediation can proceed in a number of ways depending on your situation and the style of the mediator. The first part of the process is selection of the mediator. This selection process typically happens in three ways.

First, parties sometimes elect to find a mediator even without outside motivation. With or without legal representation, parties sometimes voluntarily seek a mediator to attempt to come to agreement around one or more disputed issues.

The second, and perhaps most common, is a move to mediation after attorneys representing the parties have failed to negotiate disputed issues. There may have been a period of time during which attorneys have communicated back and forth around a disputed issue and mediation is suggested prior to filing petitions in court seeking a hearing for a judge to hear the case.

Finally, judges will sometimes order parties to go through mediation prior to issuing a final order in a case. In this situation, the court will often provide a list of local mediators who can be appointed. Sometimes the parties receive a list of three mediators one of which can be chosen by the parties.

Know that mediators are all different. It can be helpful to get input from former clients or call the mediator to ask questions prior to selection. Find out if the mediator has been performing mediation for some time or is new to mediation. How many divorces has the mediator performed? Does the mediator only address property issues, or are they experienced with matters concerning shared children? What is their style? Do they complete mediation in one long meeting, or multiple shorter meetings? Do they normally have the parties meet together in the same or separate rooms?

Will the mediator help us prepare?

Typically, there is not much communication between the parties and the mediator prior to the onset of mediation sessions. Since the mediator is not arbitrating the dispute, he or she will not need collateral data related to the issues prior to the sessions. Communication with the mediator is often limited to making logistical arrangements such as meeting time and place.

Some mediators will complete initial communications with parties to have a general understanding of the amount of disputed issues, but this is often left to the actual mediation session. Often parties will need to pay a retainer fee to the mediator prior to the onset of the mediation process. Mediation fees range from court-subsidized (or sometimes free if your local court has such a program) to $400 per hour. You may want to inquire with the clerk of your local court about subsidy programs to make mediation more affordable. This varies from county to county, but it is increasingly common for courts to have programs to make mediation more available, especially to lower income individuals.

You will usually be asked before or at the beginning of mediation to sign a contract with the mediator that clarifies their role, the fees involved, and who is responsible to write agreements if reached during the process. This contract will typically also clarify the confidentiality of the mediation process so that you understand what information will and won't be shared with outside parties or institutions. You can see a sample of such a contract here: www.mediate.com/divorce/pg39.cfm.

Some meditators will ask you to complete forms prior to mediation with information about the substance of issues you are likely to bring to the process. This is typically focused on assets and liabilities. If you have been working with an attorney, she/he may have helped you with this type of preparation. I'll discuss preparation further in the next chapter.

How many sessions?

Meetings with mediators tend to be scheduled in two ways. The most common, and most likely if your mediator is an attorney, is to schedule a long, single session. It is common for an entire day to be devoted to one meeting in which parties attempt to complete the mediation process and come to agreements.

The other style is to schedule multiple sessions of one to three hours in length. These sessions occur on separate days. Each style has benefits and complications.

Parties who participate in a single, long mediation session finish the process more quickly. This might be a benefit if the mediation is timed shortly before a scheduled court hearing. This method works best if the parties bring all necessary supportive information to the session. If the parties are well prepared, there is no need to break the process to seek additional data (for example to find out how much one person really has in their retirement account or how much equity actually exists in the house). However, long mediation sessions can be exhausting.

Because mediated agreements are often lasting, sometimes for years and of significant consequence, it would be unfortunate if parties submit to an unhelpful agreement merely due to a desire to escape a long, stressful mediation session. A bad agreement can lead to further mediation or litigation in the future. This is a common complaint I hear from parties who go through this type of mediation process. In Chapter Five, I'll explain how to best handle stress so that it not only can feel less exhausting, but so that your stress doesn't derail the process or lead to a less satisfying outcome.

Will we be in the same room?

Sometimes parties are situated at a conference table in the same room during mediation. However, it is not uncommon for parties to be in separate rooms. This is up to the mediator's preference and sometimes circumstance of the case (for example, the parties could have a restraining order which prohibits their being in direct contact). When parties are in separate rooms, this is called *shuttle mediation* because the mediator will shuttle back and forth between them.

Will we need our attorneys present during the mediation?

Some mediators have a preference about the presence of attorneys. This is a good question to have clarified prior to the start of mediation. It is often a benefit, if you have representation, to have your attorney attend the mediation. During the complex negotiations, you would have her/him available in real time to answer legal questions. Of course, inclusion of attorneys at the mediation session increases the per hour expense. If you don't have an attorney, you might still seek legal advice during or after the mediation. If you have one, it will be prudent to get consultation regarding the agreement prior to filing it with the court.

How will the agreement be written and delivered to the court?

The mediated agreement will need to be written in a way that is useful. Typically parties are mediating issues that will be entered into court petitions. You will need to clarify how the mediator will write the mediated agreement. If your mediator is an attorney, they may provide a written agreement formatted as a valid petition to file with the clerk of your court.

In that case, you will need to review the agreement, possibly with a separate attorney to make sure that it satisfies the legal requirements of the court and what the legal implications might be of the language in the agreement. If you have legal representation, you can have your attorney review the agreement prior to submission to the court.

In some cases, mediators do not prepare the agreement in legal language or a format ready for court submission. If that is true for your mediation, you will be responsible for writing the agreement into a court petition or having your own attorney do so.

Summary

After a mediator is selected, you will schedule one or more meetings. Often, this will be one long meeting during which you will attempt to finalize a comprehensive agreement. Subsidy programs may exist in your local court system to help reduce the expense of the mediation process. It is likely you will need to be prepared to pay the mediation fee at the time of mediation. It is not necessary to have your attorney present during the mediation, but the final agreement will need to be legally sound and submitted to the court in a proper format. All of these details will be clarified in a contract with the mediator before mediation begins.

PREPARING FOR MEDIATION

This chapter will help you think clearly about the issues you bring to mediation. Obviously, it would be impossible and undesirable to bring every possible issue you and the other party can think of to mediation. You also wouldn't want a court order that spelled out every aspect of life. This would be constraining and would likely set you up for being in contempt of court if you deviated later.

Sometimes people come to mediation with one very focused issue. Sometimes people have reached partial mutual agreements, but may have a small set of important outstanding disputes. Attorneys may have attempted to informally mediate these issues through communications prior to the mediation process. But, in any case, parties must choose which issues to bring to mediation. It is not up to the mediator to decided what is or isn't on the table. So, how do you sort through the many possible issues and bring to the mediation process the ones that make the most sense?

Sorting out the issues

If you use the mediation process to sort out the relevant issues (sometimes this is a useful focus for the beginning stage of mediation) you may be paying the mediator and, perhaps attorneys, for time that you could avoid. Many parties can sort out issues prior to the mediation process in order to be most clear about what to bring to the table. When I have the opportunity to help my clients prepare prior to the mediation process, I encourage them to sort out what is important and urgent and most appropriate to bring to the process.

At the point you are considering mediation, you have likely had a lot of time to think about a wide range of issues. When people are going through divorce, often they remain very highly focused on not only the strong emotions, but also many complex thoughts and worries. This strong focus results in parties thinking about much more than would be appropriate to bring to mediation. Here's one way to sort through the issues in order to choose the ones to mediate.

Importance vs. Urgency

Sort your issues by **importance** and **urgency**. Let me clarify: *Importance* means there is a consequence given a different choice around the issue. *Urgency* means if action isn't taken sooner, a different (maybe less desirable) consequence may happen. But, before you attempt this, I have to give you some bad news…

Your brain is wired to magnify both the *importance* and *urgency* of issues during high stress. This is because of a quirk of human brain circuitry called *reciprocal inhibition*. In simple terms: When some parts of your brain light up, others shut down (not completely off, but much less active). This issue applies here because:

1) *a stress reaction activates the parts of your brain designed to keep you alive when being chased by a saber tooth tiger and shuts down the parts related to thinking creatively, positively, and being future-oriented, and*

2) *divorce is, for many people, the most stressful life event ever, and this high stress lasts for months or years!*

When research has surveyed people asking about all sorts of life events and ranking them from low to high stress, divorce is always ranked as the most stressful life event. Divorce stress is also a durable type. It lasts for months and years. So my assumption for parties in divorce mediation is that they are likely as stressed as they will ever be and there is no easy escape for them…at least in the short-term.

So, part of this brain problem is that high stress is interpreted as: The building is on fire…I'm in danger! You are wired to move issues into the high importance/high urgency category, even when this is not objectively true. Here are examples of how I might sort these categories:

Low Importance/Low Urgency: *How will we divide the child's video games and toys now that we have two homes?*

Low Importance/High Urgency: *Our child is signed up for two summer camps and the deadline for a third is next week.*

High Importance/Low Urgency: *How will we schedule summer vacation next summer?*

High Importance/High Urgency: *We need to make a decision in July about where the child will attend school in August of this year. Tax forms are due soon and we must decide who will claim the child as a dependent.*

So, how do you apply this thinking to mediation? I think it is helpful in two ways. First, sorting out the issues in terms of importance and urgency can help parties choose which issues to mediate and how to approach them in the process.

Generally, I discourage parents from mediating issues of low importance, whether urgent or not. Low importance means that, even if we are fixated on a particular outcome (I really want Johnny to have the best summer possible and he should get to participate in all three summer camps...not just two!), these disputes can be avoided in the mediation process. Now, I'm not suggesting parties totally avoid addressing issues of lower importance. But, I believe that they are best addressed by mutual negotiation outside the mediation process.

As I stated before, you don't want to mediate every aspect of life that your big brain can imagine. Do you want an agreement or court order that tells you what to send in your child's school lunch or whether your child should keep a particular stuffed animal at your house or the house of the other parent? (By the way, I'm not making this up...one case I had involved parents fighting over where their six-year old daughter's stuffed animal should be. They attempted to mediate it then fought over the issue in a two-hour court hearing...spending thousands of dollars and deepening their mutual hostility.)

I think this sorting method is good to use not only for mediation, but general negotiations after divorce. One parent used a baseball metaphor to describe it well. He said, *When you're up to bat, sometimes it is best to let the ball go through and don't swing.* High stress will tend to make us swing too often. You can reduce unnecessary conflict by letting the less important issues slide and putting off less urgent issues until later.

So, actually get out a notebook. Brainstorm all the issues you're thinking about. First rank them on levels of importance, say on a scale of 1 to 10. Then, for each item, label them non-urgent or urgent. However important an issue might be, if deciding later won't change anything, then it is not urgent. And, don't count: *I'll feel better after it is decided.* If you use that justification for urgency, then everything is highly urgent. Urgency means things really do matter later in a different way. If you don't register your daughter for gymnastics by June 6th, the class will be full or closed. That's what I'm talking about.

To be clear, I'm not suggesting you avoid mediating less urgent issues. Non-urgent issues may be important to one or both parties. But, urgent issues should be dealt with first. In setting the agenda for addressing the various issues brought to the table in mediation, more urgent issues should be higher on the list.

A good way to show some empathy

Also, know that this same brain action is happening for the other party. He/she may be thinking that issues are more urgent than they objectively are. One way to handle that is to ask for clarification of the urgency. I don't suggest doing this to invalidate the other's desire to address the issue. But, if you are negotiating around which issues to address first, it may be helpful to clarify between you the objective urgency...all the deadlines...that you mutually face.

This can bolster the process by helping the other party see that you are working for mutual benefits in the agreement. They may be happy to hear you say, *I know you will need to notify your boss about summer vacation time soon, so let's figure out what our summer parenting time schedule will be.* People are more likely to shift their positions if they feel heard first. Remembering that will serve you well!

The Mediated Agreement and the Co-parenting Plan

Another way to sort issues in terms of importance is to create two separate sets of issues: one for the mediated agreement that may be entered into your divorce decree or other litigation process, and another that is a co-parenting plan that will include a wider set of issues. There are many important issues that can be clarified between parties, but which may not be necessary to define in a court order.

A co-parenting plan is an informal, but helpful, agreement between separated parents which defines agreements around issues of mutual importance. *Mom's House Dad's House* by Isolina Ricci is an excellent book which describes how to construct a co-parenting plan. Ricci explains how useful it can be to have a series of conversations about co-parenting issues (for example what in what religion parents intend to raise a child or how Little League fees will be paid) and to create an ongoing document that spells out those agreements. Another resource for brainstorming a wide range of such issues is *Building Parenting Agreement That Works: Child Custody Agreements Step by Step* by Mimi E. Lyster.

I don't think all of the issues listed in these books are always appropriate for mediation. Some are important, but best as part of an informal agreement outside the court process. One reason for this is that some issues have a lack of accountability. For example, parents might agree that they will share responsibility for taking a child to swim practice. It may be a helpful thing to spell out in a co-parenting plan. But, it may not be something to define in a specific way in a court order. It lacks accountability—a mechanism for knowing if each parent is actually doing it according to the plan. And, including too much definition in a divorce decree might invite unwarranted later litigation. You can download a good, comprehensive parenting plan worksheet at Gary Direnfeld's site: www.yoursocialworker.com. He's a social worker in Canada, but whose practice is relevant to parents everywhere. He has helpful articles on general parenting as well as issues of separated parenting. Another helpful online resource for sorting out and managing parenting time schedules is: www.ourfamilywizard.com.

What about property matters?

Your mediator may provide a worksheet to help you prepare for addressing property matters. You might also find such a worksheet at your state's government web site if you search there. You can also find such things easily with online searches. If you have been working with an attorney, you may have been guided to clarify your property issues already.

In short, you will need to know and have documentation for all assets and liabilities to be addressed in the mediation process. Parties sometimes have abstract ideas such as: We'll divide the equity in the house 50/50. If parties agree on the vague value assigned in the agreement, there may be no reason to obtain extra assessment. But there are sometimes needs to mediate the process of assigning value to an asset or debt if no objective valuation has been completed or the parties are in dispute about the value or the method by which the asset/liability was valued. For example, if no recent appraisal exists for a shared house, the parties will have to agree on a process of assigning a value for the purposes of agreeing on how to handle the equity or debt associated with it.

Summary

Brainstorm to identify possible issues, but don't bring them all to the table. Sort out the ones best addressed in the mediation process, those better served by inclusion in a co-parenting plan, and those best not addressed (at least now and as part of the negotiation process). For those you intend to negotiate, do your homework. Get objective information about property matters and deadlines for time-sensitive issues. Know that both of you are stressed out and that your brains are running interference by shifting your perceptions. But, knowing about this predictable shift can help you avoid letting it steer you into unnecessary conflict.

YOUR ATTORNEY WON'T GIVE YOU THIS

The most useful mediated agreements are satisfying now and in the future. But, however clear and helpful the agreement is to your issues, you don't want the process of mediation to interfere with your ability to negotiate with the other party in future formal and informal negotiations.

In general, people who mediate mutual agreements report greater satisfaction than those who litigate. Choosing and implementing the less adversarial approach of mediation is a good predictor of more cooperation in the complex situation of co-parenting after separation. However, while I'm an advocate of mediation, especially to avoid damaging, expensive litigation, I encourage you to think about how you approach conflict resolution (informal, mediated, or litigated) with the other party. This is especially important if you have to deal with the other party, say, as a co-parent for years to come. Let me explain...

Focus on the goals and keep the relationship in mind

When two people are engaged in conflict, they tend to be highly focused on their individual goals. If I want to borrow your car for one week and you don't want to loan it to me, my goal is to get the car and yours is to not give it to me.

But, another aspect of conflict is relationship. Regardless of the outcome of our negotiating the use of your car, the way that you and I experience negotiation will influence our future relationship. Imagine that the car is important to me right now. But, I know that you are traveling soon and I also want you to let me stay in your apartment while you are out of town. How you experience our car-related conflict will have a big influence on your willingness to participate in a negotiation with me regarding the apartment and how successful I might be with the goal of using it while you travel.

So, mediated agreements must be future oriented in this way. Surely, they are often past oriented as in: *We will divide assets earned during our marriage.* They may be present-oriented: *Now that we are separated, we both need to have sufficient assets and income to provide adequate homes for our shared child.* And, they must be future-oriented: *We need this agreement to serve us for years to come. We need it to support our becoming more, not less, cooperative so we can collaborate as co-parents and reduce our hostility. We need to avoid adversarial future conflicts, especially ones that are expensive and damaging to our relationship.*

So, in conflicts with someone whom we will have to deal with in an ongoing way, we must focus not only on the goals, but also on the current and future relationship. However, there are two issues that tend to get in the way of implementing this perspective in divorce. One is your brain and the other is your attorney.

Keep the front part of your brain online!

You remember in the previous chapter I explained that your brain is wired to have a different perspective when your stress reaction is triggered. I discussed the predictable shift in a stressed brain to interpret issues as more important and more urgent than they really are. Another predictable shift in brain function is the loss of future-oriented perspective and it happens in the same part of the brain for exactly the same reason. When that part of the brain shuts down, it is more difficult for you to take a future view of situations. It is harder to think creatively and positively when that part is less activated. For millions of years, our ancestors evolved these brains for good reason. It's not good to stop and smell the roses or think about where we might want to live next season while being chased by a saber tooth tiger! It's time to fight or flee! But, this brain function doesn't serve us so well when we need to be positive, creative, and future-oriented, even during high stress.

If I were to put you in a functional MRI machine which can provide a picture of brain activity in real time, and, I asked you to imagine going on a vacation anywhere you choose all expenses paid, the picture would show that the front part of your brain would be lit up. It is the creative, positive part of the brain. It allows us to predict future consequences and act now to promote the future that we most want. It allows us to act now in ways that, later, we are most likely to find satisfying.

So, one challenge of parties in divorce negotiations is that they walk into the meeting already at *Code Orange* or *Code Red* and then are stressed even further by the process of the conflict. So this front part of the brain shuts down. This is part of the explanation of why people involved in conflict behave in ways that are so damaging to future relationships. Their brains lose perspective. The focus is on the immediate goal (get the equity in the house) to the expense of future goals (effectively co-parent with this person for the next decade).

Get good legal advice, and use it wisely

Another challenge to this perspective is likely coming from your attorney. Now, I will tell you that I have and do work with many wonderful divorce attorneys who have a good perspective and support a wider view of getting along, especially for the sake of the children. Two ways to try to find such an attorney is to get recommendations from their former clients or to ask if the attorney has ever volunteered as a Guardian ad Litem or Court Appointed Special Advocate. These can help indicate whether the attorney is taking this wider view of helping post-divorce parents best parent children, or are interested in supporting hostile, ongoing post-divorce litigation.

But, it is not your attorney's job to help you have a good relationship with the other party. They have the role of being your zealous advocate and promoting your goals in a case. They are not failing as attorneys by remaining highly focused on goals and strategies to achieve them. I hope that you have found an experienced, competent attorney. I hope they give you useful legal advice that helps you navigate the complex legal system as it relates to your case. And, I hope very much that you use that goal-oriented advice to inform your wider perspective rather than replace it.

I will discuss in chapter seven ways to reduce stress and try to keep that front part of your brain as available as possible. But, an important safeguard is to maintain awareness of this tendency to lose wider, future-oriented perspective that pertains to maintaining a positive relationship. If you remember that, then you can try to keep this perspective as an influence in the mediation process even if it seems that everyone else in the room, including the mediator and your own attorney, has lost it. They may seem to be running interference for you, but it is your responsibility to maintain it. Losing this perspective can have damaging consequences far into the future. I'll give you an example.

A set of divorced parents came to me recently. They reported that during the first three years after their separation, they got along wonderfully. They shared a young daughter and the co-parented her cooperatively, rarely having even minor conflict. However, they had an ongoing disagreement about the parenting time schedule that they eventually decided to settle in court. They each hired an attorney and filed petitions. They went to court and got an order settling their dispute.

However, they were each so profoundly offended by the experience of the court battle (each of them felt unfairly attacked and that the other person had lied in court to try to win the case), that they no longer enjoyed a flexible, collaborative co-parenting relationship. They began fighting about things that they had never fought about before. They began fighting in front of their daughter at transitions. They then had a relationship focused on their disagreements and eventually filed more petitions to resolve a variety of disputes around issues that they had cooperated for the first three years. It was at this point that their judge refused to schedule hearings for these petitions until they sought consultation with me. It took several sessions to get them back on track and restore their prior level of cooperative co-parenting. More litigation would have only further damaged their relationship.

They were getting very good legal advice from two of the best attorneys in town. But, they got tunnel vision and focused only on their individual goals of winning the dispute at great expense. And, of course, it was their daughter who suffered most. It is not only in your best interest to preserve the relationship with the other parent, it is your responsibility as a parent to do so. While we're thinking about children, let me clarify some things about this inclusion of children in post-separation co-parenting decisions.

Keep your children out of the legal process!

We live in a society that has an urban myth that children wake up on their 12th birthday magically transformed into competent custody evaluators. Not true! Think about child development. What is the 12-year old brain up to? A common game is playing both ends against the middle. Another is getting pretty crafty at serving their selfish interests. This is normal. But, you don't want those games played out in a consequential decision around custody or parenting time.

Imagine that you walked into your attorney's office for an important consultation about an upcoming hearing to find her running out the door. On her way past you, she explains, I'm late for an important meeting with the judge, but don't worry, there's a 12-year old sitting in my office, he'll help you. Hopefully you wouldn't go in to get the child's advice. Children aren't adults. They aren't experts. They don't have life experience like adults. And, if you've been doing a good job of shielding them from inappropriate information about the divorce, your child would be operating with insufficient data to offer good advice, even if they were able (and in no way am I suggesting you inform them of all the dirty details that you would appropriately share with your attorney).

Also, when children think they are influencing parenting agreements, then they later feel responsible when there is conflict. They have more than enough divorce stress on their plate. Don't add to it. I know that some of you will completely ignore this advice. Parents who think a child will say things that support their own preferred position are often quite eager to draw the child into the process. But, it is very damaging to them. Don't do it! Again, your attorney might advise you to include the child in the process if you are on the winning end of the child's affection right now. But, I still think you must put that legal advice into perspective. You and your child must live with the consequences for a long time. Another good resource for thinking about co-parenting positively after separation is: *Good Karma Divorce: Avoid Litigation, Turn Negative Emotions into Positive Actions, and Get on with the Rest of Your Life* by Michele Lowrance.

Summary

Keep perspective. Get good legal advice. But, if you only listen to your attorney and don't keep your future-oriented and relationship-supporting perspective, you will engage in unnecessary and, potentially, damaging conflict. Aim for your goals, and act now in ways that support future relationship-goals (as in, getting along). Know that if the other party seems to be a jerk, it's because their brain has that same stress-prone wiring. And keep your children out of the process!

TO COMPROMISE OR NOT COMPROMISE?

A common dynamic between mediating parties is seeking compromise. Sometimes this is helpful to achieving mutually satisfying agreements. However, often the desire to get the other party to compromise to some satisfying extent or around a particular issue becomes the focus. Many times, this complicates, or even stalls, the mediation process. Sometimes, parties walk away with an agreement, but are not satisfied with the degree to which the other party seemed to compromise. It will be helpful to enter mediation with an understanding of compromise as a style of resolving conflict, but not necessarily the primary goal.

Let's define compromise as *a style of conflict resolution that attempts to achieve a win/win outcome*...sort of. Actually, compromise is a *win/win/lose/lose* outcome because through compromise, each party will get *part* of what they want, but also *give up part* of what they want. Imagine the following scenario...

Two parents are divorcing and mediating their parenting time agreement. Each parent wants to have primary physical custody, meaning the child will have the majority of overnights on average each year at that parent's house. After wrangling over the issue, they each decide to compromise and agree to a 50/50 split of time. The child will be at each parent's home an equal number of overnights per year.

On the face of it, this seems like a win/win situation. Each parent might be satisfied that the other parent compromised from their initial position. And, the value of fairness is supported in the 50/50 split of parenting time. Now, I'm not opposed to compromise and I'm happy if these parents are going to remain satisfied with their agreement. However, if they reached the agreement mainly because they wanted the other parent to compromise, then they might have lost an opportunity to seek an even more satisfying outcome. Let me explain by describing another scenario that was presented in another case:

Two parents were mediating, among other things, their parenting time schedule. Like the scenario described above, each wanted to enjoy primary physical custody and have the other parent follow state guidelines for non-custodial parenting. They were both motivated by the same common motivations: each wanted the most time possible with their child after the separation, and seemed (like many parents in this situation) to see gaining parenting time as a sort of win against the other parent—a expression of the overall conflict.

I have seen these conflicts over parenting time many, many times. And, one thing that is interesting is the focus on overnights. This is understandable because in many states, the number of overnights per year is part of the standard child support calculation. It is the primary way that states define parenting time schedules. And, it figures into the question of who has primary physical custody which can have significance on decision making later, even if the parties enjoy joint legal custody. It also may have tax ramifications.

So, parents are often focused on overnights as the way to define their positions and eventual agreements. I don't disagree with being clear about the relationship of overnights to those other issues mentioned above, but wider thinking can sometimes be very helpful. Back to our case…

The parents in this case had different work schedules. One parent was a manager at a business and worked a conventional Monday through Friday, 9:00-5:00 schedule. The other parent was an instructor at a local community college and taught classes at very random times through the day on various weekday and sometimes weekends. They had already decided that the parent who taught at the college would tend to be responsible for picking up the child from school even on days when he would be with the other parent. The teaching schedule provided open times to make this feasible.

I suggested that, in addition to thinking about overnights, the parents map out the hours of the week that the child would be with each parent *when not asleep*. When viewed in this manner, even with the teaching parent exercising fewer overnights, the waking hours per week were nearly 50/50. These parents became less focused on fighting over overnights and were able to establish a parenting time agreement with which they were both satisfied. If their goal had remained only to get the other parent to compromise, they might have gotten misguided from their fundamental goal of having the maximum quality time with their child after the separation.

Rather than battling over two positions and, maybe, choosing to meet in the middle, the interests that underlie the positions become the focus of the negotiation. Every position (for example, I want half of parenting time) has interests attached to it (I want a fair and satisfying amount of time with our child). Positions are strategies to satisfy interests. When people focus on interests, it is much more likely that they will achieve mutually satisfying, *win/win* agreements.

When you work with a mediator, she might ask you why you desire a certain position. This is not necessarily to challenge you or to say that you must make your position validated with a reason. But, it may be to identify the underlying interests in order to pursue a more satisfying agreement. You can use these ideas in two helpful ways.

Identify your positions and interests

First, before you walk into the mediation, do some preparation. List out the things you intend to bring to the table. These are typically positions. *I want us to choose joint custody. I want all of the equity in the house. I want to claim our child as a dependent next year.* People tend to have a variety of positions clarified in their heads long before they get to mediation.

But, I find that people are rarely fully clear about all of their personal interests that support the positions. Often the early part of my mediation process is brainstorming with clients to identify their interests in their various positions. When positions are viewed as strategies rather than the end goal, clients can become more flexible and also pursue that which is most important. I encourage you to write your positions out on paper and identify all of the interests attached to each one.

Your interests are only half of the story

Second, it can be helpful to understand the interests of the other party. You are likely in mediation because you don't agree with their position. They don't agree with yours. If you can't come to a mutually satisfying agreement, you might end up litigating which is emotionally and financially costly. Mediation is an attempt to avoid that. So, you will benefit from clarifying the interests of the other party.

I find that people who are mediating divorces often have a partial understanding of the other party's interests. However, in the best situation, they actively clarify their interests. Their somewhat educated guesses of the other party's interests come from their shared history. But, this shared history has a recent period of high conflict. This period of weeks or months (or years!) will most certainly cloud their perceptions. So, checking in about interests can be most helpful. In fact, some parties who do this might even be able to informally solve their disagreements and avoid litigation *and* mediation!

If you want the best explanations of how to effectively move to interest-based negotiation, I strongly recommend that you read *Getting to Yes:*

Negotiating Agreement without Giving In by *Roger Fisher, William Ury, and Bruce Patton* and, *Getting Past No* by *William Ury*. These books are aimed at mediators, but are easily understandable by everyone. They explain why and how to shift your negotiation style to more likely preserve good relationships *and* achieve your goals. I have recommended them to many separated parents who have found them helpful in their informal negotiations with each other around various co-parenting issues.

Summary

It is fine to seek compromise. This strategy often helps parties achieve a satisfying solution to conflict and preserve, rather than damage, an ongoing relationship. However, know that compromise is not the only way to attempt to win your goals in a mutually satisfying manner. Getting too focused on compromise can sometimes prevent people from seeing win/win solutions. Identify your interests and promote them. Your position is often a strategy to satisfy your interests, and it is the same for the other party.

HANDLING STRESS

It is no news to you that divorce is stressful. And, even if you are hopeful about the outcome of mediation, the process of mediation can be stressful, too. The bad news is that your divorce stress will continue. And, there is no magic way to prevent even the best mediation sessions from being somewhat stressful for the parties. But, there is good news. First, knowing about how stress affects you can help you control that effect, even if you can't totally make your stress go away. I'll describe, as before, how stress influences your thinking. Second, even doing small stress-relieving techniques before and during the mediation process can be of great benefit. I'll offer a few.

I have mentioned before that high stress changes the way your brain works. When the parts devoted to dealing with dangerous situations become activated, they shut down the frontal lobe, which is the part you need to think creatively, positively, and about the future. Your mind will tell you that you are seeing reality. *My ex really is a jerk! This mediator sucks! My attorney is working against me! This will never work out! I don't care what my ex thinks, I'm going to get them out of our house!* Your mind will give you ample evidence that you are right, that it's not about stress, it's true.

This effect is well-supported in countless studies in cognitive neuroscience. One one the best books out on the subject, and one which I strongly recommend for it's general benefit of promoting positive thinking and emotions, is **Buddha's Brain by Rick Hanson.** And, one which pertains directly to mediation and how to lower your stress to negotiate toward more satisfying goals is *Just Listen: Discover the Secret to Getting Through to Absolutely Anyone* **by Mark Goulston.**

Knowing about a brain effect makes it easier to cope with it. Imagine the following scenario. A sadistic researcher recruits two subjects and puts each in a separate room. Neither of the subjects regularly drinks coffee or any other caffeinated beverages. He brings each a small glass of water to which he has added the equivalent amount of caffeine as would normally be in five cups of coffee. With the first subject, he says, *Please drink this glass of water, but know that I put a large dose of caffeine in it. You'll probably feel the effects soon and they will last for quite awhile.* To the second subject, he says, *Please drink this glass of water.* (He neglects to mention anything about the caffeine!)

Which subject will experience more stress? Surely both will feel the effects of the caffeine. But the one who knows why will cope with it much better. However unpleasant the effects, she knows it will wear off eventually. She knows it's because of a drug. She knows how it got there. She was in control by agreeing to go ahead and drink the water even after she was told what was in it. The other subject will more likely flip out! She will feel the effects and not know why they are happening. She may fear she is having a heart attack or going crazy both of which are more catastrophic scenarios than I just have too much caffeine on board right now. She will not feel in control because she didn't seem to do anything to cause the symptoms.

So, just knowing that your brain is wired to work that way will actually change your stress reaction. And, remaining one degree more calm, you will have less of the effect. Knowing about it helps you cope, but causes you to have to cope with a lesser dose of stress! But, I have to be honest with you. What I'm asking you to do is a little complicated because the part of your brain you need to use to consciously remember that this effect is happening is also the part that is getting shut down by the effect. But, all is not lost.

The good news is that the frontal lobe doesn't shut off. It's not that it becomes totally unavailable. It just becomes largely shut down. You can do two things. First you can expend some effort to consciously remember that I asked you to be aware of this brain effect. Remember that, like every other human on the planet, you are wired to focus on danger in high-stress situations and ignore being creative, positive, and future-oriented. And, you can remember to do this even if it seems like your ex, the mediator, and your attorney are all running interference for you. Remember! Remember! Remember!

Second, you can do things before and during the mediation session to lower your stress. If you can come down from Code Red to Code Orange, or come down from Code Orange to Code Yellow, you will keep more of your creative, positive, future-oriented brain online.

Before you walk into your mediation session, take a few minutes (more if you have time, but even 2 or 3 minutes will be much, much better than none) to do something that relaxes you. This could be taking a walk, doing some yoga, doing some deep and relaxed breathing, getting a massage, praying (if you're religious). Do something. Really, anything, even briefly will help. If you don't believe me, I challenge you to right now relax and let out a big sigh. Do it a second time. Now do it one last time. Those three sighs probably took you less than a minute to do. But, I bet you feel a little more relaxed than one minute ago. It really works. But, it only works if you do it. I can't talk you into being more relaxed. You can only lower your stress if you do something to allow that to happen.

During the mediation session no doubt your stress will be there. As I said before, I don't have an easy way for you to make it disappear. But, you will be the best expert on your fluctuating stress level during the mediation session. Do this: right at the beginning of the session, clarify with the mediator and those present, What if I want to take a short break in the middle? Be assertive and don't think it's a stupid question. It's not a stupid question because by asking it, it really isn't so much a question as giving the others a heads up that you intend to ask for breaks during the process. It doesn't matter what you think they might think when you ask. Just ask. Then it will be easier to do so later. Your attorney and the mediator will support taking breaks because they are getting paid by the hour. More breaks means more money. The other party might not be happy about breaks if they are splitting the bill. But, my view is that spending just a few more dollars for a couple of short, five-minute breaks is going to be well worth lowering your stress and keeping more of your big brain online during the mediation.

Don't just ask about taking breaks. ***Actually take them!*** This is especially important if you are involved in a long mediation session. Take your breaks when you need to lower your stress down a notch or two. Get out of the room. Get away from your attorney who will likely just keep talking about the mediation and keep your stress level up. Get away from the mediator and the other party. Go outside. Go somewhere private. Take some deep breaths. Go touch the biggest tree you can find. Touch a big building. Touch something solid and imagine some of your stress draining into it. These breaks are not the best time to return a phone call to an angry client, or call your child's school about a behavior problem. Really take a break and get away from the mediation and get grounded. Do some deep breathing. Keep your brain online!

CONCLUSION

Think carefully about mediation. It isn't always successful. But, even if parties go on to litigate some issues, the mediated agreement can help them avoid unnecessary and damaging conflict. Mutual agreements reached through mediation are consistently more satisfying to parties than litigated issues and cost less money typically.

Use the information in this book to prepare carefully and navigate the mediation process toward the best agreements. I suggest you investigate the many resources I've mentioned in the book. And, you may want to check out your state's government web site as it likely will offer additional information about subsidy programs, mediation policies, worksheets, and links to local mediators. If you can, talk to others who have used local mediators to get input about their style and experience. Don't hesitate to ask questions of the mediator so you understand the contract and process.

Get good legal advice. But, remember to keep perspective. You need the front part of your brain online as strongly as possible because the court process, and possibly your attorney, are going to function to keep you in the adversarial frame of mind. Consider investigating local law practices that offer collaborative divorce processes which will include a mediation or quasi-mediation process to reduce conflict and save you money.

Know that even when mediation works, it is only part of your ongoing negotiations with your ex if you share children. You need to continue to work to build a functional co-parenting relationship with the other parent. Start to build a co-parenting plan that can define agreements you reach informally—outside of the mediation or litigation process.

Happy negotiating!

ABOUT THE AUTHOR

Jon Peters is a clinical social worker who has worked with divorcing parents for over fifteen years as a mediator, counselor, parent coordinator, educator, custody evaluator, consultant, and expert witness. He has delivered over 250 divorce seminars to more than 6,000 parents. An adjunct faculty member at Indiana University for ten years, he has delivered more than 80 undergraduate and graduate research, theory, policy, and mental health practice courses to students in Social Work and Applied Health Sciences. He has taught more than 40 full-semester Stress Management courses to more than 2,000 university students.

coparentingbetter.com

thrivetherapy.online